NEW TECHNOLOGY

transport technology

Brian Williams

Evans

Published by Evans Brothers Limited

© 2008 Evans Brothers Ltd

Evans Brothers Limited
2A Portman Mansions
Chiltern Street
London W1U 6NR

First published 2008

British Library Cataloguing
in Publication Data
Williams, Brian
    Transport technology. - (New technology)
    1. Transportation engineering -
    Transportation innovations -
    Juvenile literature
    2. Transportation- Juvenile literature
    I. Title
    629'.04

    ISBN 978 0 23753 429 5

Printed in China

Credits

Series Editor: Paul Humphrey
Editor: Gianna Williams
Designer: Keith Williams
Production: Jenny Mulvanny
Picture researchers: Rachel Tisdale
    and Laura Embriaco
Consultant: Dr Charles Tennant BSc (Hons),
MSc, EngD, ILTM, CEng FIMechE,
Associate Professor, Warwick Manufacturing
Group at the University of Warwick

Acknowledgements
Title page and p.21: Capoco Design; p.7
Diego Azubel/EPA/Corbis; p.9 James A.
Sugar/National Geographic/Getty Images;
p.10 Owen Franken/Corbis; p.11 Toyota;
p.13 Dane Andrew/ZUMA/Corbis; p.14
NREL; p.15 Reuters/Corbis; p.16 ZAP;
p.17 Toyota; p.18 Siemens; p.20 Siemens;
p.22 Segway Photos; p.23 Advanced
Transport Systems Ltd; p.24 Toru
Hanai/Reuters/Corbis; p.25 General Electric;
p.26 Kevin Lee/Getty Images; p.27 Mika
Grondahl/Popular Science; p.28
Americanflaghip.com; p.29
foxxaero.homestead.com; p.30 Wallenius
Wilhelmsen Logistics; p.31 Bremen Beluga
Group; p.32 Airbus; p.33 Corbis Sygma;
p.34 Lawrence Livermore Laboratory; p.35
Derimais Lionel/Corbis Sygma; p.36 U.S.
Navy; p.37 Millennium Jet, Inc./NASA;
pp.38 and 39 Lockheed Martin; p.39 bottom
Anatoly Zak; p.40 NASA/MSFC; p.41
NASA; p.42 Norsk Hydro ASA

This book was prepared for Evans Brothers
Ltd by Discovery Books Ltd.

contents

introduction   **6**

CHAPTER 1   **road** transport   **8**

CHAPTER 2   **railways**   **24**

CHAPTER 3   **all at sea:** ships and ACVs   **28**

CHAPTER 4   **air** travel   **32**

CHAPTER 5   **space**   **38**

CHAPTER 6   **the shape** of things to come   **42**

glossary   **44**

further information   **45**

index   **46**

introduction

Most people travel every day – going to work or school, for example. New technology has helped people move further and faster ever since the invention of the wheel, about 5,000 years ago. In the 21st century, people travel more than ever before. Much of this movement is by road, and in many countries the fastest area of growth is in private cars.

There are now more than one billion car drivers in the world. Yet in many cities, cars and buses go no faster than horses and carts did 150 years ago. Private transport (chiefly cars) now moves far more people on land than public transport: buses, trams and trains (see table, page 7). More cars mean increased congestion, more pollution, and more fuel used up.

Fuel Since the invention of the car in the 1880s, oil has been the world's key fuel. Current use is about 82 million barrels (1 barrel = 159 litres/42 gallons) a year. World oil reserves are estimated at about 1,000,000,000,000 barrels, though this figure includes oil deposits that are hard to reach. At present usage, experts agree the world will start

Number of vehicles in the United States 1965-present

	1965	1985	2005
Aircraft	95,000	210,000	220,000
Passenger cars	75,000,000	128,000,000	136,000,000
Motorcycles	1,382,000	5,444,000	6,200,000
Buses	314,000	593,000	795,000
Trucks (heavy)	787,000	1,403,000	2,010,000
Class 1 (mainline) rail locos	27,800	22,500	22,015
Ships (over 1000 tonnes)	2,391	748	579
Recreational boats	4,138,000	9,589,000	12,781,000

Source: US Bureau of Transportation/Britannica World Data

This chart shows how the number of vehicles in the United States has risen. Only the number of ocean-going ships and mainline rail locomotives has gone down.

to run out of oil in the mid-2000s. It will certainly become more expensive.

New technology, using new fuels, can keep people on the move. Later this century, electric cars will drive themselves on electronic highways, while giant ships cruise the oceans. Trains will zip beneath the sea in tubes,

Morning rush hour in Beijing, China's capital city. Car use in China is growing so rapidly that congestion and pollution are major concerns in the world's most populous nation and fastest-growing economy.

and robot-driver buses take people to work. In space, astronauts will build a base on the Moon.

How people in a sample of European countries travel (%)

	Car	Bus	Rail	Tram
UK	87	6	6	1
Netherlands	84	7	8	1
Hungary	60	24	13	3
France	85	5	9	1
Germany	85	7	7	1

Source http://ec/europa.eu/dgs/energy_transport/figures • 2004 data

This chart shows how most Europeans travel by car rather than by bus, rail or tram. The same is true in the United States.

CHAPTER 1
road transport

Every week, most drivers fill up their cars with petrol or diesel. These fuels come from petroleum oil. The world is running out of these 'fossil' fuels (petroleum, gas and coal). But fuel isn't the only problem. Transport also damages the environment. It can be dirty, noisy and dangerous.

Traffic-congested cities, such as Los Angeles (USA) and Mexico City (Mexico) already have serious air pollution problems. As people get richer, in countries with fast-growing economies such as China and India, they want to buy cars. More cars mean more crowded streets, more ill-health and more pollution. Making cars smaller and lighter will help – bigger cars guzzle more petrol. Travelling less helps too.

How can technology help? Science can help by developing new vehicles powered by new fuels (such as biofuels and solar power) to replace fossil fuels. Computer systems can also help to ease traffic congestion and make roads safer, cutting pollution, making the air cleaner and protecting the environment and wildlife.

Limiting car use There are more than six billion people on Earth. If every one of them drove a car every day, most roads would be jammed solid. Around the world, cities have already begun to ration car use. Bogota (Colombia) was among the first; since 1983 it has had a ban on cars in selected areas on Sunday, so the streets are free for joggers, walkers, cyclists and families with small children. San Francisco (USA) started a

CHINA'S CAR USE

China is booming, and economic growth means more cars. Car ownership in Beijing, China's capital, has doubled in five years, and will top 3 million in 2008. In the 1970s, 70% of Beijing's citizens used public transport. Today, the figure is 24%. Yet journeys now take much longer. Traffic speed has slowed, from an average 45 km/h in 1994 to less than 13 km/h today. Beijing already has 400,000 deaths a year attributed by doctors to air pollution.

Lines of vehicles wait to pay at toll booths on the Bay Bridge, in the United States. There are more cars in the United States than in any other country.

similar Saturday car-free scheme on John F. Kennedy Drive, one of the city's busiest roads, in 2007.

Traffic management Technology can help keep traffic flowing. Congestion charging in busy cities, for example, uses roadside scanners to 'read' cars passing by. Similar scanning/charging systems will become a feature of many city roads and inter-city highways. One of the first was in Singapore. Here cars are charged by electronic road pricing between set times (7.30 am to 7.00 pm weekdays). On the windscreen, the driver displays an Invehicle Unit (IU) containing a charge card, so he or she pays whenever the vehicle passes a gantry situated at numerous entry points around the city centre. The driver has a choice: pay and drive, drive another time or use public transport.

How do cars cause pollution?
Transport accounts for around 13 per cent of global warming, through the so-called greenhouse gases. This is a little less than farming, and much less than industry and power-generation, but still a problem. As a car engine burns petrol, it gives off chemicals –

THE CAR IN THE US

- 30% of the world's passenger cars are in the United States.

- Roughly 95% of American households own a car.

- More than 55% of American households have two or more cars.

- Motor vehicles in the USA burn 530 billion litres of petrol a year.

Source: World Book Encyclopedia/Britannica World Data/Wikipedia

Pointing the way to the future? This street sign in Paris, France, shows drivers of electric vehicles where to plug in to recharge their batteries.

What are alternative fuels? As the world starts to run out of petroleum, sometime this century, transport will switch to alternative fuels. There are several on the horizon. Alternative-fuel cars cause less pollution than petrol cars, but at present cost more, because they are built in small quantities.

Alternative energy sources include:

- Natural gas (in the form of compressed natural gas or CNG)

- LPG (liquified petroleum gas, usually propane or butane)

- Methane, hydrogen, nitrogen gases

- Electricity (from batteries or fuel cells, or from sunlight)

- Biofuels, from plants or microalgae.

hydrocarbons, carbon monoxide and nitrogen oxide – into the air. These chemicals are harmful to people and animals. Cars can be made cleaner. Car exhausts are already 'scrubbed' by catalytic converters, which turn the harmful chemicals into water and carbon dioxide (CO_2). But too much CO_2 is bad for global warming. Petrol cars will never be really 'green and clean'.

Cars of the future In many countries, 85 per cent of journeys are by car. Opinion surveys show that most people still expect to be driving 'cars' of some sort in 50 years' time. Tomorrow's cars will probably have wheels, but their engines will be different. Almost all cars today have internal combustion engines, burning oil. Tomorrow's cars will run on electricity or gas. Others will be hybrids, using more than one type of fuel for different speeds. Packed with electronics, the cars of the future are already starting to roll onto the roads.

The hybrid car The hybrid car has already arrived. It is more economical on fuel, because it has two engines. One engine burns petrol, the other runs on an alternative energy source such as biofuel, gas or electricity. In 2005 212,000 hybrids were sold in the US compared with about 9,500 in 2000. In 2006 Toyota sold 33 per cent more hybrids than in 2005. With rising fuel prices and increasing concern for the environment, it is expected that by 2013 hybrids will count for around six per cent of all car sales.

As hybrid cars become more common, filling stations will change. Some hybrid cars run on methane gas, for example, but the snag at present is that not many filling stations sell methane. Cars can also run on

The Toyota Prius (1997) was one of the first, and most successful, hybrid cars. It can run on just its petrol engine, or electric batteries, or use both at the same time.

HOW IT WORKS

Petrol/electric hybrid cars are more efficient than petrol-only cars, because they can store surplus energy from the petrol engine and brakes in batteries. The batteries then drive the electric engine to cut fuel consumption, and take over at low speeds (for example, in town). The hybrid car can also use solar cells to recharge the batteries when the car is not moving.

Hybrid cars use less fuel than all-petrol cars. They switch off their engines when stopped, for example at traffic lights, to save fuel. Plug-in hybrids have large battery packs that can be charged overnight. A commuter could drive 20 km to work and back, using only the electric motor, then recharge the battery overnight. With the petrol engine as back-up, there's little risk of the car coming to a halt when the power pack runs out.

HOW IT WORKS

The fuel cell changes chemical energy into electrical energy. A common type of fuel cell uses hydrogen gas as a fuel, and oxygen gas as an oxidiser (an oxidiser removes electrons, or charged particles, during a chemical reaction). The hydrogen and oxygen react in a solution of potassium hydroxide in water (this is called the electrolyte). During the reaction, electrons move between electrodes (electric terminals) inside the fuel cell, causing an electric current to flow. The current continues so long as hydrogen and oxygen continue to be added to the cell. A by-product of the process is water.

FOR AND AGAINST

For
- Hybrid cars produce less CO_2 (carbon dioxide) – a 'greenhouse gas' thought by scientists to contribute to global warming.
- Drivers benefit in some countries from lower road tax and exemption from congestion charges (London, England, for example).

Against
- Larger hybrid cars are probably not much more fuel-efficient than petrol cars.
- They cost about 20% more to buy, so not many people choose them.
- They still burn some petrol.

In a fuel cell, hydrogen (on the left) reacts with oxygen (on the right) inside the electrolyte. The hydrogen splits into +ions and −electrons. The −electrons flow through the circuit as electric current and power the motor.

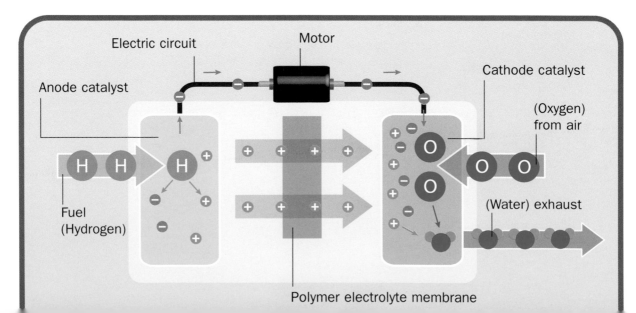

Electric circuit

Motor

Cathode catalyst

Anode catalyst

(Oxygen) from air

Fuel (Hydrogen)

(Water) exhaust

Polymer electrolyte membrane

hydrogen and nitrogen gas. So the 'petrol station' of the future will actually be a gas station.

Gas cars Future cars could run on two common gases: hydrogen and nitrogen. Liquid hydrogen can be made from water, using solar power. This is done in the BMW Clean Energy system, used to power the BMW 745h, a hybrid that has a dual hydrogen/petroleum engine. Running on hydrogen alone, it can reach 214 km/h, and has a range of 300 km. The petrol tank boosts the range by 640 km. To run its auxiliary systems, such as air conditioning, the car relies on an independent fuel cell known as a polymer electrolyte

Filling up with hydrogen at a new gas station in the United States. Hydrogen (H) is the most abundant element in the universe, and can be extracted from water. It could prove to be the fuel of the future.

membrane (PEM), which uses hydrogen from the car's gas tank.

Nitrogen can also be used in cars. It is an attractive possibility, since nitrogen is plentiful – it's the main component gas in air. The only emission from a nitrogen car is more nitrogen, so the car is pollution-free. Two prototype nitrogen cars have been developed in the United States, at the University of Washington (the LN2000) and the University of Northern Texas (the $CoolN^2$). Both use liquid nitrogen, stored at very low temperature. One problem is how to keep the freezing gas from icing up the pipes in the engine! One downside of the nitrogen car is that to make liquid nitrogen is an industrial process, requiring electrical power, possibly from fossil-fuel power plants. However, unwanted pollutant gases (such as CO_2) can be condensed and separated during the nitrogen-freezing process, and (in future) injected into used-up gas and oil wells, to prevent further air pollution. Nitrogen cars could start to have an impact during the next 20 years.

Biofuels Biofuels are fuels made from plants, such as corn and soya beans (USA), flax and rapeseed (Europe), sugarcane (Brazil) and palm oil (Asia). Biofuels can also be made from tiny living organisms, called microalgae, or

FOR AND AGAINST

For
- Biofuels are biodegradable (absorbed back into the environment). Biodiesel degrades as quickly as sugar.
- Biofuels are renewable.

Against
- More biofuels could mean fewer food crops. American farmers are being urged to grow more biofuels, so the United States buys less Middle East oil. But if too many farmers switch to biofuels, more people in poorer countries could go hungry.

Fields of fuel: rapeseed can be grown to feed farm animals, and also to provide oil for use as biofuel. Many farmers could grow fuel instead of food – but will there then be enough food to go round?

from methane (a gas that can be extracted from cow manure). Biofuels can be mixed with petroleum, to make biodiesel, which can be burned in a conventional car engine. Biofuel crops are already being grown by farmers around the world.

Solar cars Sunlight is free and renewable. It can be turned into electricity, using solar panels. Solar energy works for home-heating, and it can drive cars too. Solar cars are electric cars with an inbuilt re-charger. (They don't have to be plugged in to the main electricity supply.) As long

Solar-powered cars race at Suzuka in Japan. A saucer-shape is good for absorbing sunlight, to generate electricity for the cars' motors.

ago as 1985, 'solarmobiles' took part in the world's first race for solar-powered vehicles, in Switzerland. So why aren't the roads full of solar cars? One reason is that so far solar cars are too light and flimsy to be safe on busy roads. Solar panels (the kind seen on sun-heated buildings) are heavy. Some solar vehicles have folding solar panels which are set up when the vehicle is parked, to top up the power supply.

Astrolab, from French manufacturer Venturi, is the world's first commercial solar car (2008). Its 16-kw motor is powered by solar cells moulded into the car's carbon-based body. It has a 'sunless' range of 110 km and a top speed of 120 km/h.

WHAT'S NEXT?

In sunny Santa Monica, California, drivers of electric cars can 'top up' at a solar array of photovoltaic cells. The sunlight generates electricity in the cells to fuel the electric car chargers underneath. The filling station can handle seven cars at a time, and any left-over energy is wired into the City Hall. This could be the shape of things to come in many cities with enough sunny days in a year.

Electric cars All-electric cars have been around since the 1890s. They are clean and quiet. The two main types are battery-electric cars (power from batteries), and hybrid-electrics (a conventional petrol engine drives a generator to make electricity). Batteries have to be re-charged, and manufacturers are trying several ways of doing this. For example, General Motors' EV1 uses 'inductive charging' – the charging mechanism is outside the car, while Honda's EV+ uses a 'conductive' system – the charging mechanism is built in, and the driver runs a plug from the car to a mains socket.

Electric cars can look sporty. The Zap-X electric car has a top speed of 250 km/h, and can be recharged in only 10 minutes.

Sporty electrics The Tesla is an electric sports car launched in 2007. It is faster than many petrol cars and can run for 400 kilometres on a 4-hour charge. Powered by 6,831 lithium ion batteries, the Tesla (named after a famous scientist, Nikola Tesla) has a top speed of 209 km/h, on just two gears. It has a carbon-fibre body, so it's very strong but light. It is expensive though: US $100,000. The ZAP-X is even faster (250 km/h), thanks in part to its lightweight aluminium body. This car has four electric motors and a range of 560 kilometres.

The biodegradable car Cars are the biggest items of rubbish most people throw away. Old cars end up as scrap metal. As much as 85 per cent of a car's weight – mostly metal – can be recycled. The rest, much of it plastic, ends up as waste. In future, more of a car will be recycled.

The biodegradable car will be made from plant-plastics. One of the first is the Toyota iUnit, a prototype one-person transport revealed in 2007. Two lithium ion batteries give it a top speed of 40 km/h. Made from fibres of kenaf and lignin (natural plant materials), the car looks more like a

The Toyota iUnit, launched in 2007, is one of the most innovative transport concepts unveiled so far this century.

WHAT'S NEXT?

Future cars might be made of carbon nanotubes – tiny, thin tubes of carbon atoms. Carbon atoms 'bond' very tightly. This makes nanotubes tougher than steel, but as bendy as plastic. In theory, a nanotube car could repair itself by moving carbon atoms around to patch up holes, dents and scratches. At present, such cars are some years in the future.

foldaway baby buggy. It has two driving positions, twin joysticks instead of a steering wheel, a 'drive-by-wire' control system and proximity sensors to keep it well clear of other traffic. Because it weighs only 180 kg, it uses very little energy and when it's thrown away, most of it simply decomposes.

Safety first Today around one million people are killed in car accidents around the world every year. Rear-end collision 'beepers' are already

A 'head-up' display screen warns a driver when the car is going too fast. New technology can make driving safer, as well as less stressful.

a sign of smarter safety systems to come. Volvo has introduced a laser scanner to prevent truck collisions by slowing the vehicle; fully automatic braking to a halt is just around the corner. Alert-systems (computerised voices for example) must help drivers, without confusing them. Citroen and Jaguar sell cars with vibrating seats to wake sleepy drivers, and the Audi Q7 uses a vibrating steering wheel to warn if the car starts to veer off-road. Researchers at Oxford University found that 'multi-sensory' warning systems, like vibrating seatbelts, alert drivers faster than 'eyes' or 'ears'-only systems.

Roads of tomorrow Road engineering has already made driving safer. Examples are 'retro-reflective' paint for signs and road markings – (containing tiny glass beads to reflect car headlights); 'Fitch barriers' (barrels of sand that absorb the impact of a vehicle); and 'tone bands' or 'rumble strips' (that cause the wheels to make a warning humming noise if a driver strays towards the road-edge).

GPS satellite navigation will be developed even further, so every car's computer will pick up data from satellite traffic-watch networks, helping drivers avoid traffic jams or bad weather. GPS Satnav systems will not just follow routes but also locate any vehicle anywhere in the world. Drivers in some cities, such as San Francisco, can already check the internet for colour-coded traffic congestion maps. Manufacturers such as BMW are developing 'interactive car-communication' – if one car meets a patch of ice or fog, it will beam out a radio warning to all other cars nearby.

Smart highways, smarter cars

Many roads of tomorrow will be automated electronic routes, along which vehicles move in a regulated stream. This will involve a lot of engineering work, over the next 50 years, to install electronic guides in roads. On motorways, drivers will hand over control of the car to an onboard computer, and the car will drive itself along the electronic pathway, kept at a safe distance from other vehicles by sensors in the vehicle and in the road.

WHAT'S NEXT?

The car of tomorrow will recognise its owner by 'biometrics' – voice-recognition or eye (iris) identification. The car will start only for the right person. Seats and controls will adjust automatically to each driver's body. The car will speak to its owner, using a synthesised voice. Experts expect these features to be standard in the next 30-40 years.

This car-to-car communication system allows cars to exchange data on weather conditions. For example, if the car's sensors detect that the wipers are on (because of rain), a 'slippery conditions warning' is passed to other vehicles in the vicinity.

Four-wheel superdrive Today's cars are inefficient because a lot of the energy the engine creates is lost on its way through the car's transmission to the wheels. By the time the engine's power gets to the wheels and moves the car forward, about 50 per cent of the original power created is lost. By 2025 each car wheel will be powered by its own motor. These superwheels will have built-in steering, shock absorbers and brakes, and be able to pivot on their own. The 'eCorner' superwheel system is being developed by Siemens. Superwheels will do away with today's car engine and transmission, and be much more efficient, translating 96 per cent of the motor power into motion. New-style wheels will mean that tomorrow's cars will be able to park sideways. (Siemens already has a system called Park Mate, that can measure a parking space.) With superwheel cars, there will be fewer moving parts, fewer breakdowns and cheaper garage bills.

A cutaway diagram of the eCorner hi-tech wheel. Each wheel is powered by its own electric motor, with brakes and suspension built in.

WHAT'S NEXT?

Tyre treads (the pattern on the rubber) are designed to grip the road in rain or dry weather. In places with freezing winters, many drivers change tyres to drive on ice and snow. The Q tyre changes itself when it's icy. Retractable studs are pushed out by air pressure, for extra grip on snow. When not needed, the studs retract into the tyre.

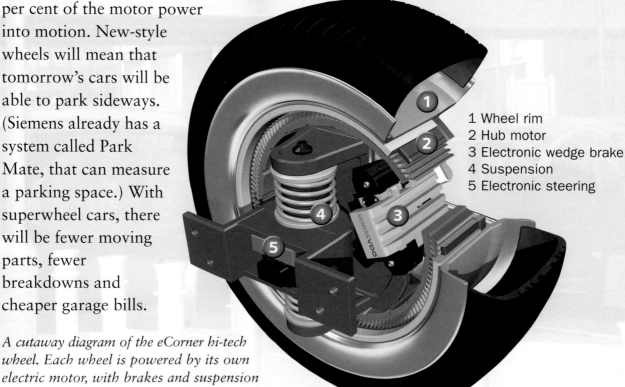

1 Wheel rim
2 Hub motor
3 Electronic wedge brake
4 Suspension
5 Electronic steering

The sound tube Noise pollution is worst around busy roads in cities. One solution is to roof over the road. This has been done in Melbourne, Australia. The city's toll-expressway system includes a stretch of 'sound tube' which reduces noise pollution close to high-density housing. The tube acts as insulation, to shut off the noise from people nearby. Sound tubing could become a feature of inner city roadbuilding in other countries too.

City transport By 2012 Londoners could be riding on a driverless 'pod-bus' which follows magnets in the road. The bus navigates using a system called FROG – short for 'free ranging on grid'.

London could see these caterpillar-like 'pods', alongside the city's familiar double-decker red buses. Above the street is a train on one of the city's overground rail links, the Docklands Light Railway.

A grid of magnets in the road guides the bus along its route, and controllers can follow its progress on an electronic roadmap. Passengers call the bus from a mobile phone and the bus can redirect itself to collect them from pick-up points along the route. A prototype robot bus is due in 2008, with a system up and running for the 2012 Olympics. Pods will be linked up to form trains.

Hybrid buses For fuel economy, the 'pod-bus' will have an electric/biofuel hybrid engine. Hybrid buses are already at work in cities around the world, for example in Seattle and New York City (USA), Valencia (Spain) and Mexico City (Mexico). London began testing double-decker hybrid diesel/electric buses in 2007. The buses offer a 30 per cent cut in pollutant gas emissions. In typical operation, a diesel/electric bus switches from its 'hush mode' electric motor at low speed (below 24 km/h) to a diesel engine for faster speeds between stops.

Bamboo bikes Over the past 50 years, more people have used cars, and fewer people have walked or ridden bikes. Yet walking and cycling are sutainable (no fuel is burned), healthy and beat congestion. Many cities encourage bikes, through cycle lanes and pedestrian zones. An interesting alternative to the conventional bike

WHAT'S NEXT?

Power-walking aids could speed up trips to the shops or school. Take the Segway, a 'personal transport device' unveiled in the early 2000s. It has two wheels driven by electric motors and computers and gyroscopes for balance. By leaning forwards or backwards, the rider makes the 'walker' go faster or slower. The Segway tilts backward (to slow down) when nearing its top speed of 20 km/h. It also slows or stops if it touches an obstacle. The Segway has had its problems, and not everyone believes it is the answer to getting around a city, but it's fun to try.

American police in the city of Baltimore go on patrol riding Segway 'walkers'.

(made of metal, plastic or carbon fibres which are expensive and non-renewable) is the bamboo bike, invented by Brazilian engineer Flavio Deslandes. Bamboo grows rapidly. It is cheap and renewable. It is light, but as strong as steel in some situations.

People-moving People-movers or Personal Rapid Transits (PRTs) are the next step from elevators, moving pavements and escalators. They are ideal for moving people around airports and shopping centres. One of the first was the Never Stop Railway, built for the British Empire Exhibition at Wembley, London, in 1924. A total of 88 carriages ran on a circular track, using a screw-thread propulsion system, never

A passenger prepares to board an ULTra car at London's Heathrow airport. ULTra is one of the first automated people-moving systems.

stopping. Passengers stepped aboard a carriage as it slowed to walking pace. The Jacksonville Skyway system in Florida (USA) was completed in 2000. Carriages run in trains along a 4-km track. There are two newer systems: ULTra at Heathrow Airport, London, and one at Dubai, both starting in 2008. PRT systems could become common in cities, to help ease urban congestion alongside light railways, trams, monorails, robot buses and electronic roadways.

HOW IT WORKS

The ULTra system is a bit like a theme park ride with small electric cars on wheels running along a guideway. On ULTra, passengers wait just a few seconds for the next car. Each car seats four people and travels at up to 40 km/h.

CHAPTER 2
railways

Railways can carry more passengers and haul more freight than any other form of land transport. They can match aeroplanes for fast journey-times between city centres (planes have to drop off their passengers at airports, usually many kilometres from the city).

Trains cause less air pollution than cars and trucks. GPS tracking means controllers know the location of every locomotive and freight wagon. ECP (electronically controlled pneumatic) brakes help make train travel very safe.

Developments in hi-tech trains include new power sources, improved vehicle and control systems to allow for faster trains and more trains on existing tracks, and automated rapid-transit systems.

Will future trains go faster?

France, Japan and Germany led the way in high-speed trains (HSTs). New HSTs won't be much faster than the French TGV, which set a world speed record of 515 km/h in 1990. Some HSTs use tilting rolling stock,

A new Japanese N700 'bullet train' slows down as it enters Tokyo station. These are the first Japanese bullet trains able to tilt around curves without slowing down.

HOW IT WORKS

Building new track costs a lot of money. To carry more passengers on existing track, a railway can operate longer trains. This is being done on London's Jubilee Line (Underground). Trains can run closer together, thanks to new electronic signal and control systems to ensure safety. On commuter lines, double-decker carriages double capacity, though this may mean raising the roof of tunnels built in the 19th century for steam trains.

to take bends on old track at high speed; an example is the N700 Shinkansen in Japan, due to start running in 2009. It uses less energy than earlier HSTs, accelerates faster and has improved aerodynamics for a quieter, more comfortable ride at up to 300 km/h. Japanese-built Javelin trains will run shuttle services into London on the new high-speed line, for the 2012 Olympic Games. They will run at 225 km/h. California plans a high speed line that will run services between San Francisco and Los Angeles in just under two hours.

Hybrid trains Most trains today are diesel-electric (oil-burning engines drive electricity generators) or electric (the current comes from overhead wires or an electrified third rail). A hybrid locomotive runs on diesel, but converts energy from its brake system into additional energy, for motion and for storage, in electrical batteries. A pioneer hybrid loco, in 2002, was Green Goat, a Canadian shunting/switching machine locomotive that gets 85 per cent of its energy from 336 two-volt batteries. It's clean too. It produces less than 20 per cent of the gas emissions of other diesel locomotives.

General Electric's Evolution is a US hybrid diesel-electric locomotive. It converts energy released from its braking system into electricity, to boost its performance and reduce exhaust emissions.

Cyclists pedal beneath one of Shanghai's maglev trains, which speed at up to 400 km/h along a 65-km track to and from the Chinese city's airport.

Maglev trains 'Maglev' is short for magnetic levitation. Maglev trains 'float' above a metal track, and are pushed along by a linear motor. Propellers or even jet engines could also be used to propel the train. With no wheels rubbing on rails, there is little friction so maglev trains are very fast. Experimental German and Japanese maglev trains have reached 550 km/h per hour. The first operational maglev railroad opened in Shanghai, China, in 2002. It runs out to the airport on 30 km of track at speeds of up to 500 km/h.

FOR AND AGAINST

For
- Maglev trains are very fast.
- They cause little pollution.

Against
- They are expensive to build.
- Maglev trains generate between 62-90 decibels of noise, higher than most intercity trains. Compare that with trucks at around 65 decibels or jet aircraft at 105 decibels.
- The strong EDS magnetic field could affect passengers with electronic heart pacemakers, as well as computer drives and credit cards.

Rapid transit Trains underground are also the subject of new technology. New York City, along with other cities, plans to upgrade its subway system. By 2050, new trains will use Communication Based Train Control (CBTC). Transponders between the rails will link electronically with the trains, providing instant communication between each train unit and the control centre. Trains will run faster, closer together and more safely. In future rapid transit systems, individual cars will operate on their own, forming trains and uncoupling at stations to head off on another route. Standby cars will join trains automatically at peak times. Every seat might have a computer terminal so the passengers can work, play, watch a film or just keep in touch.

This diagram shows how a vacuum tube train will run through a tunnel, anchored to the ocean floor.

WHAT'S NEXT?

Sucking air out of a tube (to make a vacuum) means there is no friction. A train running inside a vacuum tube could reach 3,000 km/h. This is envisaged by two ex-Massachusetts Institute of Technology engineers, Ernst Frankel and Frank Davidson. In their futuristic design, the trains run through tunnels suspended up to 90 metres deep in the Atlantic Ocean. By 2050, vacuum-tube trains could whizz from London to New York in two hours, faster than a plane today.

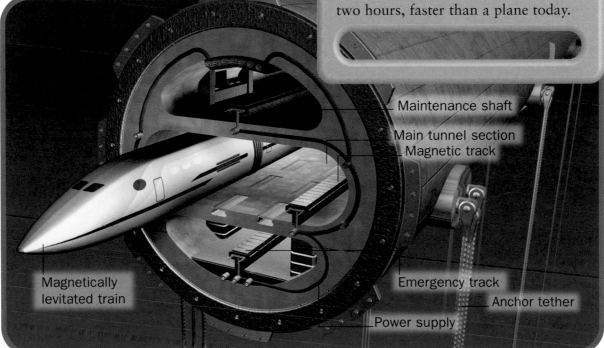

Maintenance shaft

Main tunnel section
Magnetic track

Magnetically levitated train

Emergency track

Anchor tether

Power supply

CHAPTER 3
all at sea: ships and ACVs

Ships are getting bigger all the time, especially cruise ships. *America World City*, a supergiant cruise liner (planned by World City Corporation, USA), will be one of three supergiant ocean liners: 250,000 tonnes and 380 metres long. It will carry 3,000 passengers and 1,500 crew. Future floating hotels could be as big as cities.

A proposed mega-giant US vessel called *Freedom* will carry 50,000 people. More than 1,220 metres long and 2.7 million tonnes, it will be a motorised island, with its own marina, airstrip and railway. Instead of a hull, 600 air-tight cells will act as the foundations for the 'city' on top.

Making containers go faster Most sea-freight is shipped inside box-like containers. Big ships carry more than 9,000 containers and usually take up to 25 days to journey between Europe and the United States. The

HOW IT WORKS

The ADX Pentamaran will carry around 1,000 containers across the Atlantic Ocean at around 85 km/h. Its ultra-thin hull will cut through the water, supported by four outriggers, like those on a catamaran.

An artist's illustration of the America World City, *the world's largest passenger ship, which will feature a planetarium, tennis courts and a 2,000-seat theatre.*

ADX Pentamaran, a proposed hi-tech container express, will do the trip in three days. Designed by British engineer Nigel Gee, the ship will have jet engines to push it through the water faster than all but a few specialised vessels.

Wingships Wingships are vehicles that skim the waves. Hovercraft or air-cushion vehicles (ACVs) can travel over land or water. Wingships are bigger and faster, but can only move over water. They are also called 'wing-in-ground-effect' (WIG) ships. They look like seaplanes about to take off, but never fly. Instead, they skim the water at over 480 km/h.

The proposed Atlantis *wingship would represent a major engineering breakthrough. It would be 10 times bigger than any ground-effect vehicle so far built.*

HOW IT WORKS

As a plane lands, it seems to 'float' in the air just before touching the runway. The plane seems to rest on a cushion of air, like an ACV. The cushion is produced by the plane's forward motion. A wingship makes use of this effect. It does not need air-blowing fans and a 'skirt', like an ACV.

WHAT'S NEXT?

The biggest WIG so far was the 'Caspian Sea Monster'. It was 132 metres long and weighed 500 tonnes. A new type of wingship, *Atlantis*, would be ten times bigger: 5,000 tonnes. Outline designs show that it would carry 30 times the payload of a Boeing 747, and cross the sea at 750 km/h, but it remains to be seen whether it will ever be built.

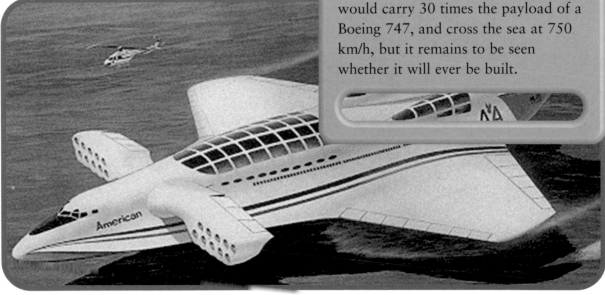

Do electric ships work? At least 13 navies, including the US Navy, are planning all-electric ships. The electric ship uses a gas turbine, or a nuclear generator, to generate electricity for motors to turn a propeller. Another system uses propulsion pods. These are electric motors, each attached to a short propeller shaft and fixed to the outside of the hull. Pods are lighter and easily serviced. Electric ships can also go backwards as easily as forwards – useful for docking in port.

Sail power Hi-tech sails make sense for big ships, as well as yachts. The *E/S Orcelle*, a 2005 cargo-ship design by the Wallenius Wilhemsen company of Scandinavia, will be a 'green' ship: 'E/S' means environmentally sound. *Orcelle* will use electric power, through variable speed propulsion 'pods', and also tap into wave power and the wind. It will use fuel cells to make electricity, and three rigid sails, which will

SHIP POLLUTION

- Ships carry 75% of world trade, but produce less air pollution through greenhouse gases than cars.
- Ships use less than 3% of the fossil fuel we burn. However, most fuel burned by oil-burning ships is 'bunker fuel', the dirtiest form of oil.

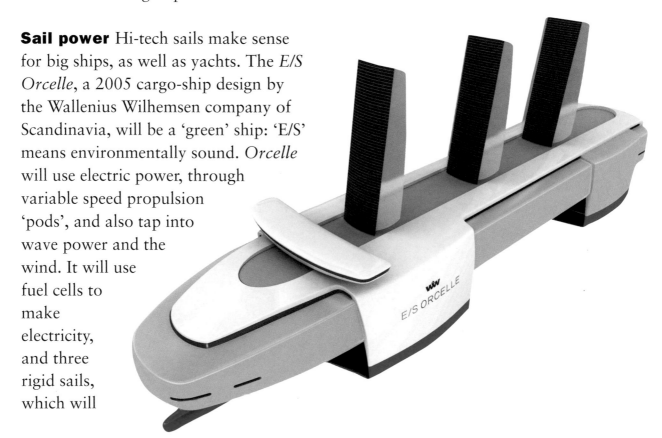

A model of Orcelle, a revolutionary 'zero emission' ship. With its mix of power sources, Orcelle (named after a dolphin) will use only renewable energy, the first to do so since the big sailing ships of the 19th century. The funnel-like structures are rigid sails, covered in solar panels.

catch the wind and contain solar panels too. *Orcelle*'s underwater fins will convert wave energy into more power.

The kite-sail Ever been pulled along by a kite in a strong wind? The kite-sail, a concept from the German company SkySails, looks like a giant paraglider. It is flown above a ship and tugs the ship along, saving up to 50 per cent on fuel for part of the voyage. The first ships with kite-sails took to the seas in 2007, beginning with the Bremen-based Beluga SkySails.

A ship being towed by a kite-sail. The sail is made of chambers filled with compressed air. It is tethered by steering lines to a cable. The cable can move along the side of the ship as the wind shifts direction.

FOR AND AGAINST

Wind-ships: could sails make a comeback?

For
- Fuel accounts for around 60% of the cost of running a big ship. Wind is free and clean. Ships could use kite-sails, as 'extra' propulsion units.

Against
- Wind power is unreliable. With no wind, a sailing ship stops. Most sailing ships are too small to carry much freight.

CHAPTER 4
air travel

More people fly every year. Airports get bigger and busier. Aeroplanes burn a lot of fuel – thousands of litres on each flight. Jet engines contribute to global warming and air pollution through carbon emissions.

At present rates of growth in air travel, aeroplanes will use up all the planned reductions in greenhouse gases in other areas (such as factories, cars and houses) by 2050. Cars and planes contribute to global warming through carbon emissions. One survey, from the Edinburgh Centre for Carbon Management, reports that three return flights from London to New York (roughly 33,500 km) emit 1,000 kg of carbon per person. That's about the same as a year's driving in an average car, around 1,100 kg of carbon.

Bigger jumbos The airline business is dominated by two big companies: Boeing (USA) and Airbus (Europe). The Airbus A380 is a 'super jumbo', which carries 555 people. It is an updated version of the classic jumbo jet. Instead, Boeing's hi-tech 787 Dreamliner, rolled out in 2007, seats half as many people but Boeing claims its hi-tech design, using carbon fibre instead of traditional metal-alloy, makes the Dreamliner lighter and more fuel-efficient. It also means it can have larger windows, giving passengers a better view.

Passengers try out the seats in the wide cabin of the Airbus A380, the world's newest and biggest jumbo jet.

WHAT'S NEXT?

The 'flying wing' triangular shape for aircraft was first tried in the 1940s. It's now called a 'blended wing body' (BWB). A flying wing flies well at high altitude. An experimental flying wing, the Boeing X-48B, could lead on to the first commercial BWB airliner by 2020.

Why no new Concorde? Very fast fighter planes fly at Mach 3 (three times the speed of sound), but carry only one or two people. Most airliners (with up to 350 passengers) fly at just under Mach 1 (Mach 1 is the speed of sound). That's roughly 965 km/h – about half as fast as Concorde. Like all supersonic aircraft, Concorde made a 'sonic boom' (caused by shock waves in the air). The noise meant Concorde was banned from flying supersonic across the United States. This hit sales. Only 16 Concordes were sold to airlines.

NASA drew plans for a new High Speed Civil Transport (HSCT), a supersonic airliner quieter and cleaner than Concorde, but it has not been built because so far engineers can't beat the sonic boom problem. So new airliners, like Boeing's proposed Sonic Cruiser, will still fly at Mach 0.98 (so no 'sonic boom'). A plus for the Sonic Cruiser is its very long range: over 18,000 kilometres non-stop.

Boeing's Sonic Cruiser will fly at almost the speed of sound. Were it to fly supersonic it would produce 'sonic booms' – noises clearly audible on the ground – and the plane would face objections from environmentalists.

Skipping around the Earth

HyperSoar is a design from Lawrence Livermore National Laboratory in the United States for a dart-like plane that will fly at Mach 10 – 10,782 km/h. It will 'skip' along the edge of the Earth's atmosphere, like a pebble across a pond. HyperSoar will climb to 39,640 metres, then turn off its engine to glide down. Its next engine 'burn' will send it soaring back up again. And so on, until it comes down to land like a normal aeroplane.

Synthetic vision

In space-planes like HyperSoar, passengers probably won't have windows. Instead, they will get a virtual view, with a synthetic vision system (SVS), already being introduced to help pilots and ground controllers. SVS provides a clear-screen image, even in fog. Like the simulated landscape in a computer game, it generates a three-dimensional colour picture. As GPS satellite navigation tells the SVS system where it is, the virtual view changes all the time.

An artist's rendition of what HyperSoar will look like. It could be built in the next 10-15 years.

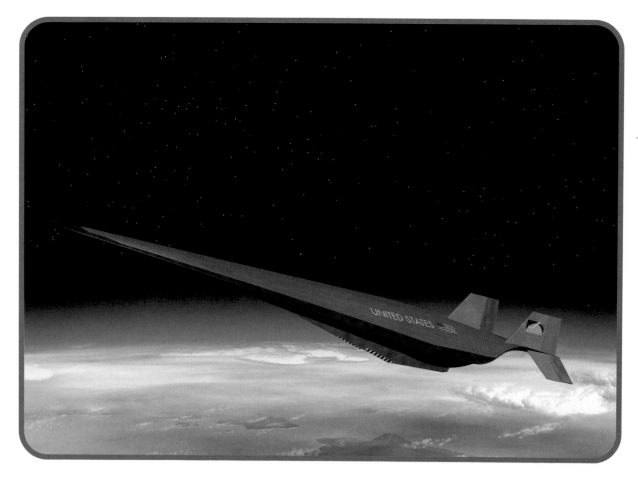

Return of the airship? In 1936 the hydrogen-filled German airship *Hindenburg* crashed in flames in America. This tragedy seemed to end the airship era. However, the airship could make a comeback. Airships are slow, flying at not much more than 160 km/h. But they are good for lifting cargo. They can fly long distances and they give passengers a great view. Modern airships are safer, because their 'lifting' gas is helium, which does not catch fire. Airships currently flying include helium and hot-air versions. The prototype of a very large cargo airship, the German *CargoLifter*, was flown in a small-sized version in 1999. If and when the full-scale airship is flown, it will be as big as the 1930s *Hindenburg*, and carry 160 tonnes of freight over several thousand kilometres.

Inside a 360-m long hangar near Berlin, Germany, engineers are working on a new generation of airships. The helium-filled CL160 CargoLifter is designed to carry a payload of 160 tonnes. The airship has eight engines: four for propulsion, and four for manoeuvres while flying.

Electric aeroplanes Electric planes can be powered by current from fuel cells, or sunlight (solar energy). The world's first fuel-cell powered airplane is the French DynAero Lafayette, an experimental propeller plane tested in the early 2000s. James Dunn, US pioneer of the laptop computer in the 1980s, is one of the inventors hoping to build more electric aircraft, including one called 'Electra-Plane'.

Electric motors are quiet and clean, but electric planes are not likely to replace jets yet. They're too slow. But

The solar-powered airplane Helios, *photographed over Hawaii during its first test flight under solar power (2001).*

HOW IT WORKS

Solar-powered microlights could be the 'air cars' of tomorrow. *Helios* is an experimental US solar-powered plane, developed by NASA. It has already flown 30 km high, without a pilot. It has 14 electric motors turning 14 propellers, and 62,000 fuel cells to collect sunlight. For the time being, it is just experimental, with no passenger flights in view. *Helios* is not much faster than a bicycle. It's too light and flimsy to carry passengers. But because it runs on sunlight, a solar plane could in theory stay in the air for weeks at a time.

fuel cells could replace auxiliary power units (APUs) in airliners. These units power a plane's electrical and air systems on the ground. Fuel cells could produce twice the power, for the same fuel cost.

Air-scooters Personal fliers or air scooters look fun in sci-fi films. SoloTrek is a VTOL (vertical take-off and landing) air-scooter that can fly at 128 km/h, hover like a helicopter and has a range of over 160 kilometres. The

Solotrek is an XFV (Exo-Skeleton Flying Vehicle in NASA jargon). A joint NASA/Millennium Jet project, this one-person flying machine has two ducted fan engines and a top speed of around 100 km/h.

idea is to produce an aeroplane that is cheap, easy to fly, to provide people with a 'bird's-eye view' whenever they want one – checking farmstock maybe, or surveying land.

Convertiplanes Airliners need long runways. Runways take up space, so most airports have to be built kilometres from city centres. V/STOL (vertical/short take off and landing) planes could fly passengers from city centre to city centre. One solution is a convertiplane: half-helicopter, half-plane. The idea was tested in the 1950s, by the British Fairey Rotadyne. It had a big rotor (like a helicopter) but wings with engines for forward flight. The US Osprey tilt-rotor aircraft has the same V/STOL capability, tilting its rotor-propellers through 90 degrees to change from vertical to horizontal flight. It's a military plane, but a civilian version could operate in and out of city centre airports – if it's not too noisy.

Gyrodynes The Groen Hawk 4 gyrodyne (2000) is a US convertiplane. It can take off and land in less than eight metres. It has a top speed of 240 km/h. The US Groen company has plans for larger convertiplanes, with rotors like the 1950s Rotadyne; these projects include the Gyrolifter transport and the Gyroliner commercial carrier.

CHAPTER 5
space

The US Space Shuttle will be retired from space in 2010. A new generation of manned spacecraft will then take astronauts and tourists into space. The United States, Russia, China, Japan and the European Space Agency are all building new spacecraft.

Orion *Orion* is the new US manned spacecraft. *Orion* will fly to the International Space Station, and by 2020 will be ferrying astronauts to the Moon.

This artist's impression shows Orion *with the Lunar Lander in orbit above the Moon. Like in the Apollo missions, the Lunar Lander is the separate craft used to land on the Moon.*

HOW IT WORKS

Orion will be launched on top of the *Ares* rocket. Similar in shape to the 1960s Apollo spacecraft, *Orion* is three times bigger inside and packed with 21st century microelectronics. For Moon flights, it will join up in space with a Moon-landing module. *Orion* will carry six astronauts. *Orion* will re-enter the Earth's atmosphere for a splashdown landing in the sea.

Ares: successor to Saturn *Ares 1* will launch *Orion*. The Ares rocket will lift a payload of 25,000 kg into Earth's orbit. *Ares 5* will be bigger, as big as the *Saturn 5* Moon rocket of the 1960s – 110 metres high. *Ares 5* will lift 127,000 kg. These rockets will become operational between 2010 and 2020.

This is the version of Kliper that is being developed with wings, but a wingless version may still be produced.

The Ares 1 *launch vehicle will launch the new* Orion *manned spacecraft, which will replace America's Space Shuttle.*

WHAT'S NEXT?

Kliper ('Clipper') is a new Russian 'lifting-body' spacecraft proposed for the 2020s. A lifting body is a wingless aeroplane. It is shaped like a cone cut in half. The shape gives it 'lift' when flying like a plane in the atmosphere. Although simple to fly in space, lifting body craft are hard to fly in the air and land. So Kliper may be given stubby wings so it can glide down onto a runway like the Shuttle. If it ends up wingless, it will be landed by parachutes. The European Phoenix and US X-33 are other lifting body spacecraft under development.

Space tourism In 2004, *SpaceshipOne* made the world's first privately-funded space flight: 100 kilometres into space, though not into orbit. By 2009, *SpaceshipTwo* should be carrying space-tourists from Virgin Galactic's spaceport in New Mexico, USA. A second spaceport is planned for Sweden. The folding-wing, two-pilot spacecraft will be lifted beneath a mother-plane, *White Knight Two*, then rocket away at 4,000 km/h, to give six passengers a thrilling glimpse of space during a 2-hour trip.

Solar voyages Rocket motors burning chemical fuel (liquid hydrogen and liquid oxygen) are inefficient and slow, in space terms. Alternative propulsion systems for spacecraft include electric propulsion (using the Sun's energy); the electricity is used to generate an ion-drive gas stream. The first ion-drive spacecraft was NASA's *Deep Space* probe (1998). For voyages to the edge of the solar system and beyond, solar sails could be the answer for the mid 2000s. There is no air or wind in space; a solar sail is 'blown' by the solar wind, a stream of light particles (photons) moving out from the Sun. A solar-sail spacecraft

A solar sail spacecraft, as it would look in orbit above the Earth. The mirror-like sails are made of material up to 100 times thinner than a sheet of writing paper.

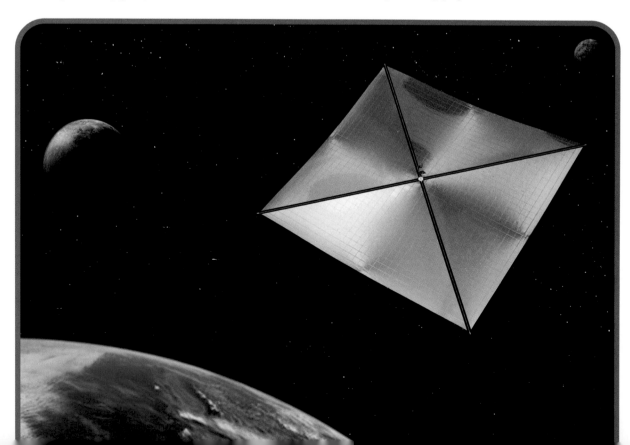

WHAT'S NEXT?

How about riding into space in a space elevator? The idea of an orbital tether, like a very long cable reaching into space was suggested by Russian scientist Konstantin Tsiolkovsky at the beginning of the 20th century. It could happen by 2050. To make the tether, a rocket would carry the cable from a launch tower to a space station in orbit 240-320 kilometres high. Space elevators would then travel up the tether, by maglev propulsion, and transfer passengers and freight to the space station, with no pollution, and cheaper than rocket launches.

would accelerate to 322,000 km/h. It could sail to the edge of the solar system in eight years – compared with the 40 years for the *Voyager 1* space probe, launched from Earth in 1979 and still outward bound.

NASA's proposed space elevator. Electromagnetic space vehicles will travel up and down the elevator, which will be geostationary – it will keep the same position relative to the ground as the Earth rotates.

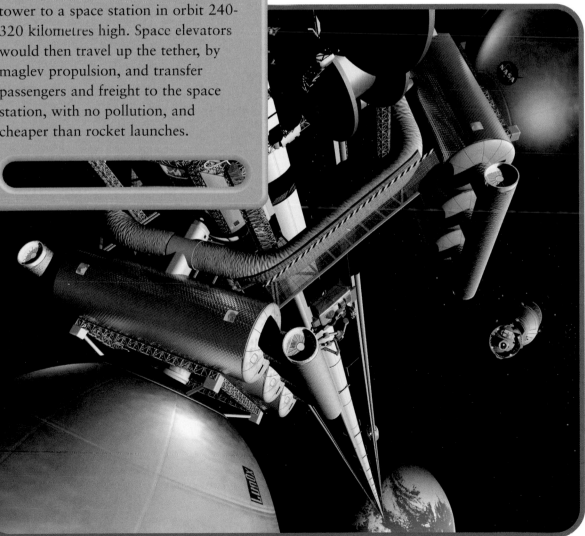

CHAPTER 6
the shape of things to come

Transport is a growth industry worldwide. There will be perhaps 10 billion people by 2050. More people will travel in and around cities, and (unless air travel is restricted) more people will want to fly between countries. More goods will be shipped around the globe, by sea, rail and road. This growth poses problems: cost, congestion, accidents, pollution, fuel shortage and environmental damage.

Green transport In future, many people may choose to travel less – working at home more, by computer. But most surveys show that travel will keep on growing in the next 50 years. By then the world's reserves of fossil fuels will be practically used up. So before 2050, a new generation of

Iceland, which already gets 72 per cent of its energy from geothermal and hydroelectric power, could be the world's first hydrogen-based economy. By 2050, all the country's vehicles could be hydrogen-powered, like this bus.

vehicles will be in use, powered by alternative energies.

Public transport will provide one answer to overcrowded roads. Public transport was for many years underfunded, as people switched from buses and trains to private cars. That's starting to change. While some cities, like Curitiba in Brazil, have built integrated transport systems, encouraging bus use over many years, others face severe transport problems, caused by rapid growth. In Mumbai (India) for

WHAT'S NEXT?

By 2020, astronauts will be building a base on the Moon. The base is likely to be built near one of the Moon's poles, in the hope of using sunlight there for solar power and lunar ice as a water supply. The first missions to the Moon will send robots to find landing sites, survey natural resources and reduce possible risks in time for the arrival of the first astronauts. Four-person crews will then begin making seven-day visits to the Moon until their power supplies, lunar vehicles and living quarters are up and running.

instance, rail planners are replacing 8-car trains with 12-car trains, just to cope with the extra passengers.

Integrated transport Integrated transport systems link up all the strands of a transport system. Technology helps to keep travellers informed, so they can switch from car to bus to train to plane, and walk or cycle when they wish. Road-pricing and rationing systems (like the one in Singapore) will become more sophisticated. People will get used to paying to drive, just as they've got used to park and ride systems in towns.

The ideal integrated transport system does not yet exist. In Genoa, Italy, the transport system already involves a mix of alternatives: controlled car access, two funicular railways, a metro (underground), hybrid and electric buses, a dial-up taxi service and methane-fuelled minibuses. London, England will have new transport links in place for the 2012 Olympics.

Travelling safely Technology must also protect travellers – by making vehicles safer, and by improving security systems. Security has become a major issue, particularly at airports and rail stations. Today security checks make air travel a time-consuming business. However technology in this area is improving all the time, spurred on by international efforts to combat terrorism and prevent transport crime.

Into the future By 2050, most cities will have a mix of transport systems. There will be new shapes in the sky (like airships), on the water (like wingship freighters) and maybe underwater (like cargo-carrying nuclear submarines). This book has mentioned a few of the exciting possibilities. Some are already here; others just over the horizon. Whatever happens, the 21st century will see a lot of changes to the way people get around.

glossary

ACV ACV stands for 'air-cushion vehicle'.

aerodynamics Study of the forces acting upon aircraft or other machines travelling through the air.

airship Floating powered aircraft, filled with a lighter-than-air gas such as helium.

biodegradable Able to be broken down by bacteria.

biofuel Any fuel made from plants.

biometrics Identification of a person by biological features, such as voice or eyes.

catamaran Water craft with twin hulls.

container ship Freight ship carrying cargoes packed inside large metal boxes that can also be carried on trucks.

diesel Heavy oil used in diesel engines (named after German engineer Rudolf Diesel, 1858-1913).

drive-by-wire Technology which replaces the traditional mechanical and hydraulic systems with electronic control systems.

ELV Stands for 'expendable launch vehicle', a multi-stage rocket.

fossil fuels Oil, gas and coal, formed millions of years ago in the Earth's rocks.

fuel cell Chemical device for making electricity.

gas turbine Engine in which hot gases turn the blades of a turbine wheel at great speed.

GPS Stands for Global Positioning System, the global satellite navigation system.

greenhouse gases Gases such as carbon dioxide, ozone, methane and nitrous oxide, believed to contribute to the greenhouse effect, or 'global warming' when they build up in the atmosphere.

ground effect Extra aerodynamic lift from a 'cushion' of air trapped beneath a vehicle such as an ACV or wingship.

HST Stands for High-Speed Train.

hybrid Vehicle with two kinds of engine.

hydrocarbons Chemical compound of hydrogen and carbon, formed when fossil fuels are burned.

paraglider Flying machine like a box-shaped parachute, with air-filled wings.

payload The passengers, cargo or bombs carried by an aircraft.

sonic boom A loud noise created by supersonic aircraft. Sonic booms sound like explosions and may exceed 200 decibels. Thunder is a natural type of sonic boom.

TGV Stands for Train à Grand Vitesse (High Speed Train, in French).

transponder An electronic device that picks up a signal and automatically reponds to it. The magnetic labels on credit cards are examples of transponders.

further information

Books

Dilemmas in Modern Science: Power by Kate Ravilious, Evans Brothers Ltd, 2008.

Science Essentials Chemistry: Fuels and the Environment by Denise Walker, Evans Brothers Ltd, 2007.

Aircraft: Technology All Around Us series by Kay and Andrew Woodward, Franklin Watts, 2005.

Amazing Machines: Mighty Cars by Ian Graham, Franklin Watts, 2006.

Websites

Lots of interesting articles on robotics, gadgetry, concept cars, space and computer games.
www.21stcentury.co.uk

Website that explains how many new machines work.
www.howstuffworks.com

Learn about the history of space flight and future space programmes.
www.nasa.gov/audience/forstudents/index.html

Places to visit

Greater Manchester Museum of Transport
www.gmts.co.uk

Hovercraft Museum Trust, Lee-on-Solent, Hampshire
www.hovercraft-museum.org

Imperial War Museum, Duxford
www.duxford.iwm.org.uk

London Transport Museum
www.ltmuseum.co.uk

Merseyside Maritime Museum
www.liverpoolmuseums.org.uk

Museum of Science and Industry in Manchester
www.msim.org.uk

Museum of Transport, Glasgow
www.glasgowmuseums.com

National Maritime Museum, Greenwich
www.nmm.ac.uk

National Motor Museum, Beaulieu, Hampshire
www.beaulieu.co.uk

Portsmouth Historic Dockyard
www.historicdockyard.co.uk

RAF Museum, Cosford, Shropshire
www.rafmuseum.org.uk

Scottish Maritime Museum
www.scottishmaritimemuseum.org

index

Numbers in *italic* refer to illustrations.

ADX Pentamaran 28-29
air-scooters 37
Airbus A380 32, *32*
aircraft 6, 32-37
airships 35, *35*
America World City 28, *28*
Ares rocket 38, 39, *39*
Astrolab 15
Atlantis 29, *29*

bicycles 22
biodegradable cars 17, *17*
biofuel 8, 11, 14, 22
biometrics 19
Boeing 747-400 32
Boeing Dreamliner 32-33
buses 6, 21, 22
BWB aircraft 33

CargoLifter 35, *35*
cars 6, 7, *7*, 8-20
catalytic converters 10
CBTC systems 27
China 8
computers 18-19, 27
Concorde 33
congestion charging 9, 12
convertiplanes 37

DynAero Lafayette plane 36

electric vehicles 7, 11, 12, 15, 16-17, *16*, 22, 25, 30-31, *30*, 36-37, 40
Evolution train *25*

FROG systems 21
fuel cells 12, *12*, 13, 30, 36, 37
fuel reserves 6, 8, 42

gas cars 11, 12, 13, *13*, 14
global warming 9, 10, 12, 32
GPS Satnav 18-19, 24, 34
Green Goat locomotive 25
gyrodynes 37

Helios 36, *36*
HSTs 24-25
hybrid vehicles 10, 11, *11*, 12, 22, 25, *25*
hydrogen power 12, 13, 42
HyperSoar 34, *34*

Iceland 42
integrated transport systems 42-43

Jacksonville Skyway 23

kite-sails 31, *31*
Kliper 39, *39*

maglev propulsion 26, *26*, 41
Moon 38, 39, 43
motorcycles 6
motorways 19

N700 trains *24*, 25
nanotube cars 17
NASA 33, 36, 37, 40, 41
nitrogen fuel 13, 14
nuclear power 30

oil 6, 9, 30
Orcelle 30-31, *30*
Orion 38-39, *38*
Osprey tilt-rotor 37

petrol 8, 9, 10, 11, 12, 13, 14
pollution 8, 13, 14, 21, 22, 24, 26, 30, 32, 41

Q tyres 20

rail travel 6, 7, 24-27
roads 18, 19

safety systems 18-19, 43
sailing ships 31
Segway 22, *22*
ships 6, 7, 28-31
solar power 8, 11, 13, 15, *15*, 16, 31, 36, *36*, 40, *40*, 43
SoloTrek 37, *37*
Sonic Cruiser 33, *33*
sound tubing 21
space 7, 38-41, 43
space elevator 41
SpaceShipTwo 39
supersonic aircraft 33
SVS vision 34

traffic 6, 7, 8, 9, *9*, 18, 19
trucks 6

ULTra system 23, *23*
underground systems 25, 27

vacuum trains 27, *27*
VTOL 37, *37*

wave energy 31
wheels 20, *20*
White Knight Two 40
wingships (WIGs) 29, *29*

ZAP-X 16, *17*